Contents

Macmillan Education
4 Crinan Street
London N1 9XW
A division of Macmillan Education Limited

Companies and representatives throughout the world

Ferris Wheel 3 Student's Book ISBN 978-1-380-01868-7
Ferris Wheel 3 Student's Book Pack ISBN 978-1-380-02677-4

First published 2019

Original design by Clare Webber
Page make-up by emc design ltd.
Illustrated by Jose Ignacio Gómez (Nacho Gómez) pp3–100 (all character artwork and main illustrations), 101–112 (Mimi).
Other illustrations by Animation Group Sp. z o.o. pp101–112; Conor Rawson (Beehive Illustration) pp12, 24, 26, 36, 38, 48, 50, 60, 62, 72, 74, 84, 86, 96, 98.

Cover design by emc design ltd.
Cover illustration by Jose Ignacio Gómez (Nacho Gómez) with additional artwork by Conor Rawson (Beehive Illustration).
Picture research by Lorraine Beck.

Author's acknowledgements
I would like to thank everyone at Macmillan Education in the UK, Spain and Mexico who has contributed to the development and production of these materials. I would also like to thank all the teachers who have taken time to read and pilot the materials, and given invaluable feedback at every stage of writing the course. Special thanks as ever go to my husband, Alan, for his encouragement and support, and to our son and daughter, Jamie and Hannah, from whose early childhood days I learnt so much.

The publishers would like to thank Alex Tamulis, São Paulo, Brazil; Ayşegül Sezer, İNO Schools, Turkey; Daniela Araujo Pielli, Alt Idiomas, São Bernardo Do Campo, Brazil; Daniela Pugliese, Milton's College, Buenos Aires, Argentina; Esra Ezici, Turkey; Fernanda Domeniconi Nery Amorim, São Paulo, Brazil; Gabriela Iocolari, English Schoolhouse, Buenos Aires, Argentina; Gulbin Cin, Bahcesehir College, Turkey; Mariana Pastorino, Em Pi Instituto de Inglês, Santa Fe, Argentina; Mariné Ortiz, Warrington, Buenos Aires, Argentina; Paola Daniela Tuninetti, Academia Argüello, Córdoba, Argentina; Silvana Paola Accardo, Escuela Cooperativa Mundo Nuevo Instituto Casa de Jesús, Buenos Aires, Argentina.

Printed and bound in Brazil.
2025
49

The authors and publishers would like to thank the following for permission to reproduce their photographs:

Alamy Stock Photo/Frankie Angel p36(dinner), Alamy Stock Photo/Stefan Ember pp35, 43(brushing hair), Alamy Stock Photo/Freer Law p74(card tubes), Alamy Stock Photo/GeoStills p81(butterfly), Alamy Stock Photo/Victor Gladkiy p16(trees), Alamy Stock Photo/Esa Hiltula pp15, 23(merry-go-round), Alamy Stock Photo/Idea studio pp55, 56, 63(pool), Alamy Stock Photo/IMAGEMORE Co. Ltd pp35, 43(brushing teeth), Alamy Stock Photo/James Jackson p36(breakfast), Alamy Stock Photo/Juniors Bildarchiv GmbH p81(eggs), Alamy Stock Photo/David Lee p46(tl), Alamy Stock Photo/Roel Meijer pp15, 23(slide), Alamy Stock Photo/Monkey Business p29(parrots), Alamy Stock Photo/Pixavril p101(sticker – painting), Alamy Stock Photo/Apisit Sriputtirut pp25, 29, 33(crocodile), Alamy Stock Photo/Anna Stowe pp55, 63(toyshop), Alamy Stock Photo/Martin Sudzina pp81, 83(caterpillar), Alamy Stock Photo/Wavebreak Media Ltd p56(zoo), Alamy Stock Photo/John White Photos p59(m), Alamy Stock Photo/Sergey Yarochkin p74(yoghurt pots), Alamy Stock Photo/Zoonar GmbH pp46, 49(spaghetti); **Getty Images** pp26(monkey), 31(t), Getty Images/ac_bnphotos p46(pizza), Getty Images/ AlasdairJames pp51, 53(crisps), Getty Images/Ale-ks pp75, 76, 79, 83(ladybird), Getty Images/AlexStar p84(modelling clay), Getty Images/Steve Allen p59(l), Getty Images/allFOOD p103(sticker – rice), Getty Images/aluxum pp51, 53(plums), Getty Images/ amriphoto pp25, 26, 29, 33(elephant), Getty Images/aopsan p54(plate), Getty Images/artisteer p36(lunch), Getty Images/bgfoto pp16(grass), Getty Images/ David Bishop Inc. pp45, 53(chicken), Getty Images/brentmelissa pp65, 69, 73(maracas), Getty Images/Carlsson, Peter p56(restaurant), Getty Images/cenkertekin pp15, 23(seesaw), Getty Images/ChiccoDodiFC p39(preschool), Getty Images/cjmckendry pp15, 16, 23(pond), Getty Images/Clover No.7 Photography pp11, 13(running), Getty Images/CT757fan p74(colored paper), Getty Images/DarioEgidi p56(supermarket), Getty Images/Peter Dazeley p36(shower), Getty Images/Dorling Kindersley pp65, 69, 73(recorder), Getty Images/Elva Etienne pp5, 13(drawing), Getty Images/EyeEm/Vesna Jovanovic p51(icecream), Getty Images/EyeEm/Alexander Palm p51(market background), Getty Images/EyeEm/Adzahar Saini pp15, 23(swing), Getty Images/EyeEm/Kazuki Tsune p81(chrysalis), Getty Images/fanjianhua p16(path), Getty Images/ FatCamera p11(cr), Getty Images/Floortje pp45, 53(pancake), p46(br), Getty Images/fotoedu p74(sellotape), Getty Images/Stephen Frink p59(r), Getty Images/GalapagosFrame pp16, 19, 23(bench), Getty Images/GlobalP pp25, 33(hippo, lion, parrot), p26(hippo, parrot, snake, zebra), p29(monkeys), Getty Images/GrashAlex pp65, 69, 73(tambourine), Getty Images/hallojulie pp19, 23(park), Getty Images/Hemera Technologies pp14, 24, 64(paper), Getty Images/Hero Images pp55, 63(museum), Getty Images/HHelene pp75, 76, 79, 83(bee), Getty Images/ImagesBazaar p11 (cl), Getty Images/Image Source p39(house), Getty Images/indigolotos p49(bl), Getty Images/iStockphoto p26(giraffe), 45, 46, 53(yoghurt), 65, 69, 73(guitar), Getty Images/iStockphoto/Thinkstock pp29(hippo), 74(rice), Getty Images/ithinksky p51(peas), Getty Images/Juanmonino p46(fish), Getty Images/Kaphoto p76(ant), Getty Images/KidStock pp35, 43(getting dressed), Getty Images/Dave King pp45, 46, 53(toast), Getty Images/ kivoart p49(br), Getty Images/kk2s pp65, 69, 73(piano), Getty Images/kristianbell pp31(b), 33(br), Getty Images/Philippe Lissac pp5, 13(counting), Getty Images/losw pp16, 19, 23bmr(merry-go-round), Getty Images/luamduan p26(tiger), Getty Images/lucielang pp34, 44, 64(crayons), Getty Images/magnetcreative pp51, 53(oranges), Getty Images/malcolm_grima pp75, 79, 83(snail), Getty Images/Rob Maynard p56(park), Getty Images/MilaDrumeva p101(sticker – bench), Getty Images/monkeybusinessimages pp35, 43(washing hands), 55, 63(movie theater), Getty Images/Marvin E. Newman pp55, 56, 63(shops), Getty Images/Neyya pp11(tl), Getty Images/photohampster p16(flowers), Getty Images/photka p16 (seesaw), Getty Images/pioneer111 pp16, 19, 23 bmr(swings), Getty Images/Raffalo pp75, 79, 83(worm), Getty Images/RedHelga p51(carrots), Getty Images/RuthBlack p51(cupcakes), Getty Images/Serg_Velusceac pp14, 24, 74, 84(paints), Getty Images/Sergiy1975 p16(slide), Getty Images/Sidekick p11(tr), Getty Images/somethingway pp5, 13(singing), Getty Images/Spaces Images p56(bookstore), Getty Images/Chris Stein p11(bl), Getty Images/travellinglight p46(soup), Getty Images/Udomsook pp44(pencil), Getty Images/Martin Wahlborg p16(park background), Getty Images/Wavebreakmedia pp35, 43(getting up), Getty Images/ YinYang p69(drum), Getty Images/Priscila Zambotto pp5, 13(building); **Getty Images Plus/**iStock pp45, 53(lettuce); **iStockphoto/**alex_kz pp14, 24, 34, 44, 54, 64, 74, 84(glue); **MACMILLAN MEXICO/**Tony Sanchez pp75, 76, 83(butterfly); **Springer Nature Limited/**Paul Bricknell pp5, 13(coloring), 102(sticker – washing face); **Shutterstock**/Serhii Bobyk p56(cinema), Shutterstock/Chursina Viktoriia pp51, 53(candy); **Spectrecom** pp9, 12, 13(bmr), 22, 29(c), 32, 33(bmr), 39(tr), 42, 43(bmr), 49(t), 52, 59(tr), 62, 63(bmr), 69(c), 72(tr), 73(bmr), 79(tr), 82, 83(bmr); **www.imagesource.com** p34(string).

Commissioned photos by Helen Marsden/Spectrecom pp4, 6, 7, 11(Alex,Lucy,Auntie Vicky), 14(1,2,3), 16(Alex and Lucy), 17, 19(tr), 21, 24(1,2,3), 26(Alex and Lucy), 27, 31(tr), 34(wool,tissue paper,hanger,1,2,3), 36 (Alex,Lucy), 37, 41, 43(br), 44(1,2,3), 46(Alex,Lucy), 47, 51(Alex,Lucy,Auntie Vicky), 53(bmr), 54(tissue paper,1,2,3), 56(Alex and Lucy), 57, 61, 63(br), 64(1,2,3), 66, 67, 71, 72(Alex,Lucy), 73(br), 74(tissue paper,stickers,1,2,3), 76(tr), 77, 81(tr), 84(tissue paper,1,2,3).

Hello
How are you?

1:17 1:19 hello

Listen and sing *Ferris Wheel*. Listen, point and say. Stick the number stickers. Circle your favorite number. Ask and say. Language: Mommy, Daddy, Mimi, Dylan; Ferris Wheel; blue, green, orange, pink, red, yellow; numbers 1–6; Hello. How are you? I'm fine, thank you. Where's number (one)? It's on (red).

Lesson 2 Story

1:20

hello

Watch. Listen to the story *Hurry up, Mommy!* Circle and color the items Mimi and Dylan give Mommy. Ask and say. **Language:** apple, hat, shoes, shorts, socks, T-shirt, water; late, sleepy; Hello. How are you? I'm (sleepy). Hurry up. Here's your (hat). Goodbye.

School

A new friend

Listen, point and repeat. Listen and stick the school activity stickers. Listen and play *Memory*. Circle the activities you like. Say. Language: color, count, draw, paint, play, sing; blue, green, orange, pink, red, yellow; Where's (draw)? It's on (red).

Language

Listen and find the new school activities. Listen, point and sing *What do you do at school?* Match the activities to Lucy and Alex. Ask and say. **Language:** count, dance, draw, jump, paint, run, sing, think; What do you do at school? I (draw) at school.

Lesson 3 Story

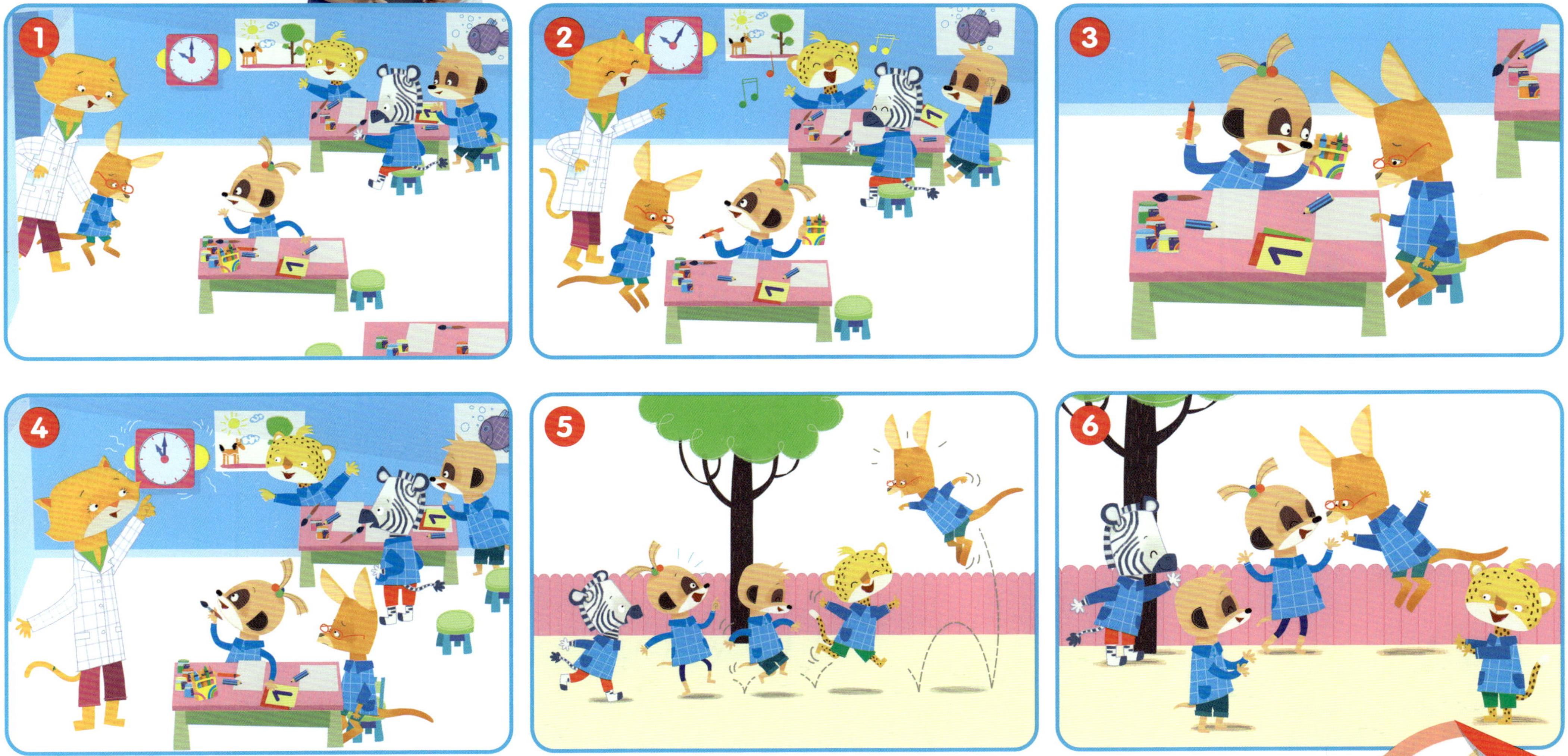

Watch. Listen to the story *A new friend*. Circle who's new at school. Stick the story sticker.
Language: color, count, dance, draw, jump, paint, run, sing, think; What do you do at school? I (think) at school. Do you want to (color)? Yes, I do. / No, I don't. I want to (jump).

Lesson 4

Story Song

Watch. Listen, point and sing *Katy Kangaroo*. Trace ✔ or ✘ to show what Katy does and doesn't want to do. Trace and color Katy. Ask and say. **Language:** color, count, draw, jump, paint; Do you want to (draw)? Yes, I do. / No, I don't. I want to (jump).

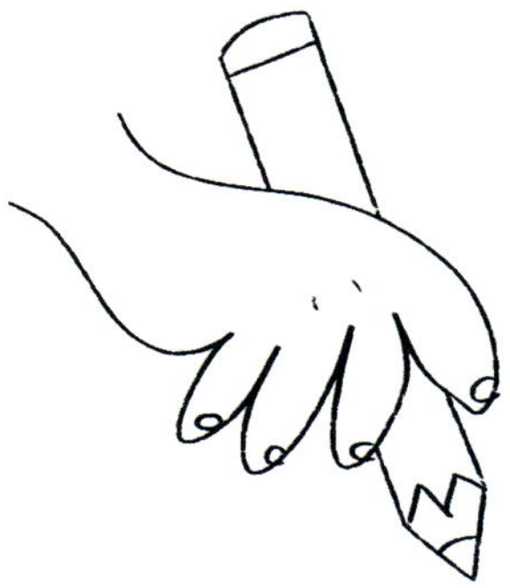

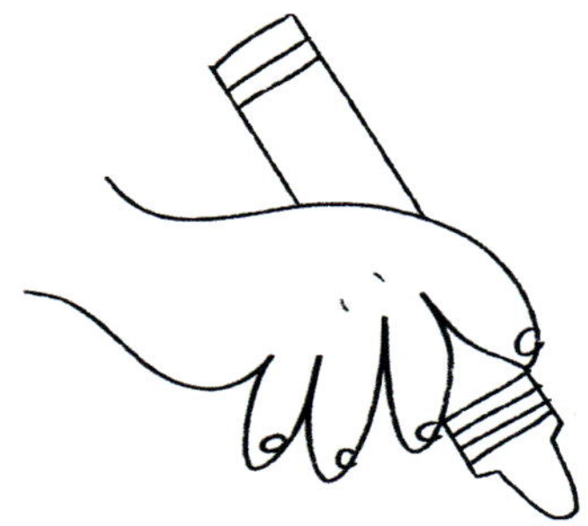

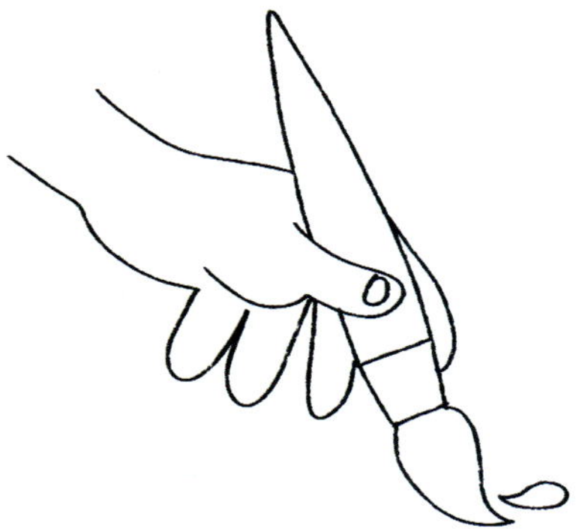

1:30

hello

Watch. Listen and point. Circle what Alex and Lucy want to do. Color what you want to do. Ask and say. Language: color, dance, draw, paint, play, sing; Do you want to (paint)? Yes, I do. / No, I don't. I want to (play outside). I don't want to (draw).

Lesson 6

Values Being kind

Listen and point to the story. Say. Color the child being kind at school.

Language: color, help, play, share, sit down; bag, banana, coat, crayons, friend, home, school; happy, sad; Do you want to (play)? I like/don't like (school). I'm (happy). I want to (go home).

SOCIAL AND EMOTIONAL LEARNING

Content

Listen and point. Match the activities to Auntie Vicky, Alex and Lucy. Circle the exercise you do. Ask and say. Language: dance, play soccer, ride my bike, run, swim, walk (to school); What exercise do you do? I (play soccer).

Culture

School

1 2 3 4

1:33

Watch. Listen, point and sing *Go in and out the window*. Match and number the photos in order.
Language: dance, go, shake hands, stand; partner, window; numbers 1–4

Review

I can …

Vocabulary

Story

Speaking

Content

Circle the school activities you know. Listen, point and say. Listen and answer. Ask and say. Complete the faces to show what you can do. **Language:** color, count, dance, draw, jump, paint, play, run, sing, think; What do you do at school? I (draw) at school. Do you want to (sing)? Yes. / No. I want/don't want to (color).

Project

COOPERATIVE LEARNING

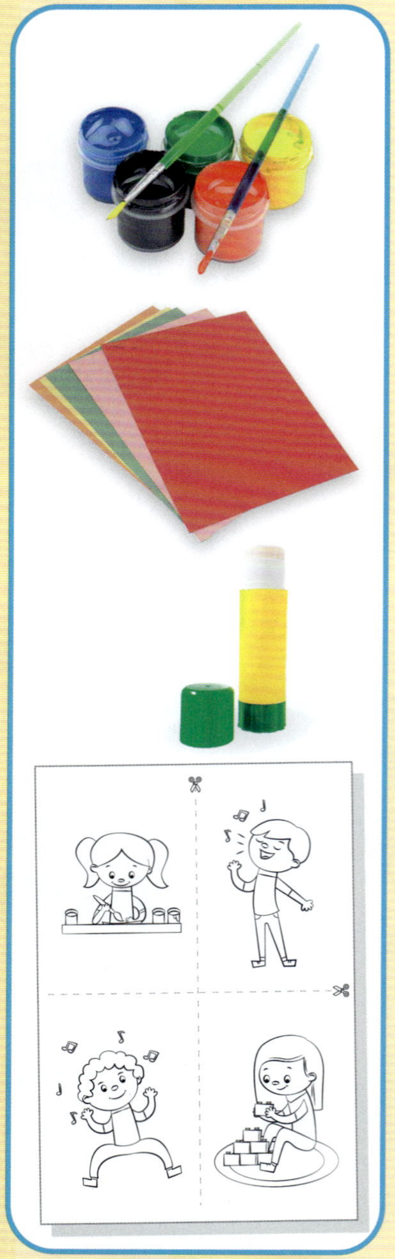

1

2

3

Choose and paint your favorite school activity. Glue your picture on the chart. Ask and say. **Language:** dance, paint, play, sing; colors; numbers; chart; What do you do at school? I (dance) at school. How many people (dance)? (Four). Do you want to (paint)? Yes, I do. / No, I don't. I want to (play). I don't want to (sing). I like the (blue) pictures.

The park

Mimi's kite

Listen, point and repeat. Listen and stick the park stickers. Listen and play *Memory*. Circle the things in your park. Say. **Language:** bench, merry-go-round, pond, seesaw, slide, swing; blue, green, orange, pink, red, yellow; Where's (the seesaw)? It's on (pink).

Language

The park

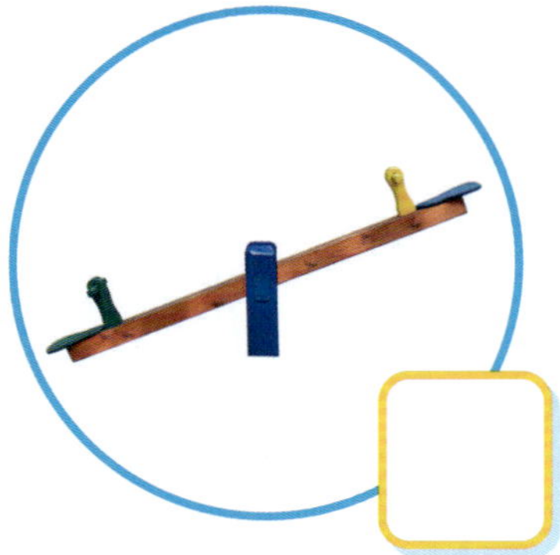

1:39 1:40 hello

Listen and find the new park words. Listen, point and sing *There's a pond in the park*. Check (✓) the park objects in the song. Say. Language: bench, flowers, grass, merry-go-round, path, pond, seesaw, slide, swings, trees; There's (a pond). There are (trees).

Story

1:42

Watch. Listen to the story *Mimi's kite*. Circle the weather in the story. Stick the story sticker.

Language: bench, flowers, kite, path, pond, slide, swings, trees; windy; It's (windy). There's (the pond). There are (the flowers). Is there (a slide)? Are there (swings)? Where's (Mommy)? Under (the tree). On (the bench).

Lesson 4 Story Song

The park

1 2 3 4 5

Watch. Listen, point and sing *Fly the kite*. Trace the numbers. Match the numbers and pictures in order. Say. **Language:** flowers, kite, pond, trees; numbers 1–4; There's (the pond). There are (the trees).

Lesson 5

Speaking

Life skills

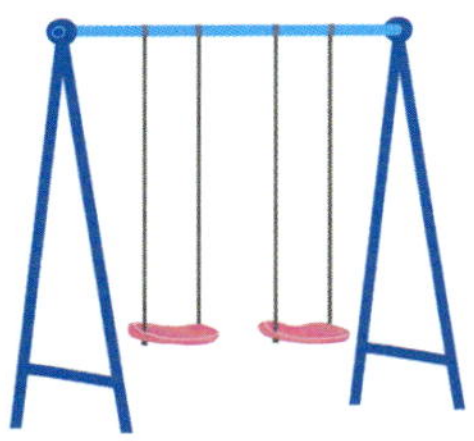

Watch. Listen and point. Circle what's in the park. Ask and say. Language: bench, flowers, grass, merry-go-round, path, pond, seesaw, slide, swings, trees; Is there (grass)? Are there (trees)? Yes. / No. There's (a merry-go-round). There are (swings).

Values Looking after the environment

The park

1:46 hello

Listen, point and sing *Put your trash in the trash can*. Trace and color the trash can black. Find and match the trash to the trash can. Say. Language: park, trash, trash can; clean; Put your (trash) in (the trash can). I put my trash in the trash can.

Lesson 7 Content

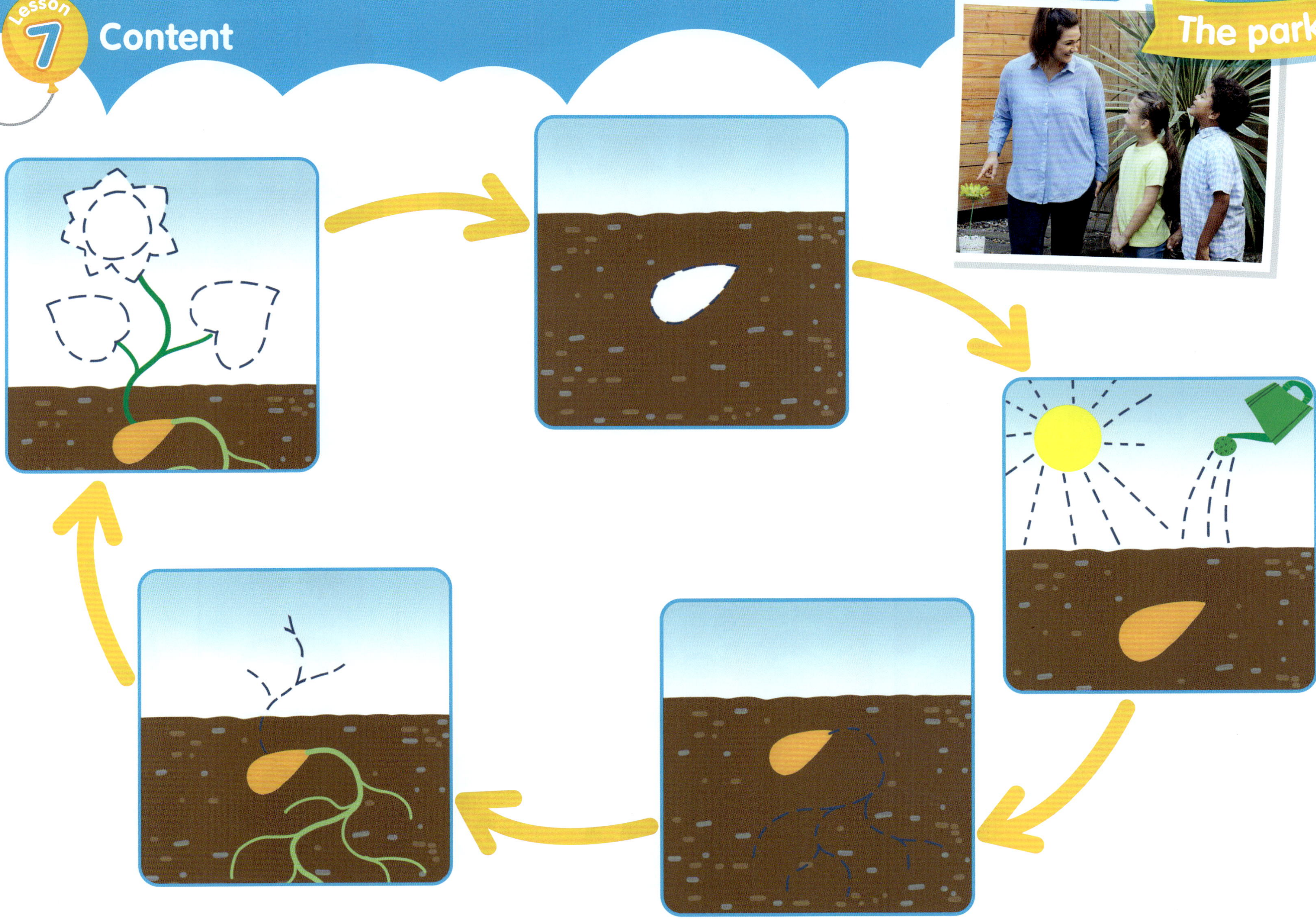

Listen and point. Trace and color the pictures to show the life cycle of a plant.
Language: flower, leaves, plant, roots, seed, sun, water; There's (a seed). There are (leaves).

Lesson 8 Culture

Watch. Listen and point to the story *Little Red Riding Hood*. Circle the words you hear in the story. Say. **Language:** apples, cake, cookies, ears, eyes, flowers, house, path, teeth, trees, wolf; There are (trees).

Review

I can ...

Vocabulary

Story

Speaking

Content

Circle the park words you know. Listen, point and say. Listen and answer. Ask and say. Complete the faces to show what you can do. Language: bench, flowers, grass, merry-go-round, path, pond, seesaw, slide, swing, trees; What's in the park? There's (a pond). There are (flowers). Is there (a slide)? Are there (swings)?

Project

COOPERATIVE LEARNING

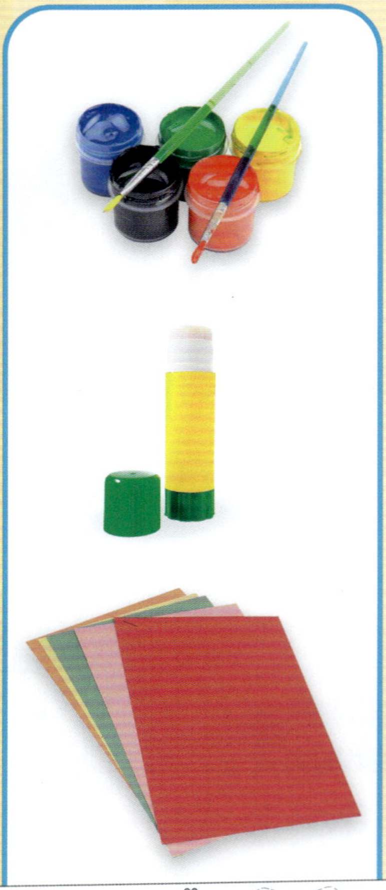

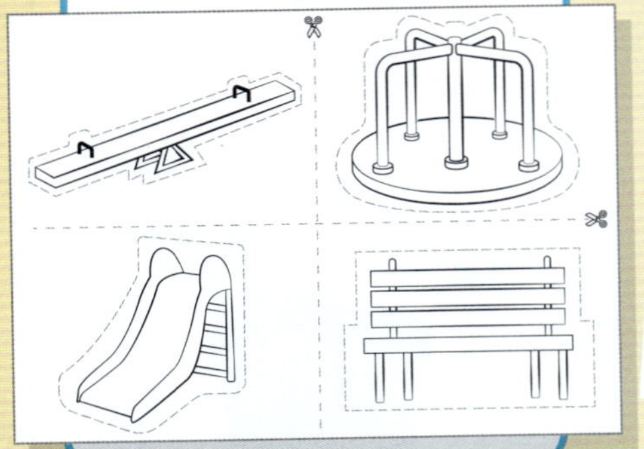

Choose and paint an object for the park. Glue your picture on the model of a park. Ask and say. Language: bench, merry-go-round, seesaw, slide; colors; numbers; There's (a slide). There are (seesaws). Is there (a bench)? Are there (flowers)? How many (trees)? (Six.) My (slide) is (red). I like (the merry-go-round). Do you like (the slide)? Yes. / No.

Wild animals

The surprise

Vocabulary Lesson 1

Listen, point and repeat. Listen and stick the wild animal stickers. Listen and play *Memory*. Circle the animals you like. Say. Language: crocodile, elephant, hippo, lion, monkey, parrot; blue, green, orange, pink, red, yellow; Where's (the crocodile)? It's on (green).

Language

2:04 2:05 hello

Listen and find the new wild animals. Listen, point and sing *What's that?* Check (✔) the animals Alex and Lucy see. Ask and say. Language: elephant, giraffe, hippo, monkey, parrot, snake, tiger, zebra; colors; What's that? It's (a snake). It's (black and white). It has (big teeth).

Story

Watch. Listen to the story *The surprise*. Circle Mimi's birthday present to Dylan. Stick the story sticker. **Language:** binoculars; crocodile, lion, monkey, parrot, snake, tiger; colors; What's that? It's (a tiger). It's (orange and black). It has (big eyes). I'm (a crocodile).

2:07

Lesson 4

Story Song

Wild animals

2:08 hello

Watch. Listen, point and sing *The party surprise*. Match the animals to the characters. Circle your favorite animal and character. Ask and say. Language: crocodile, lion, monkey, parrot, snake, tiger; What's that? It's (a snake). I'm (a tiger).

Speaking

Life skills

Watch. Listen and point. Check (✓) the wild animals Auntie Vicky, Alex and Lucy see at the safari park. Draw a wild animal you want to see. Ask and say. Language: crocodile, elephant, hippo, monkey, parrot; What's that? It's (an elephant). It has (big ears). What are those? They're (monkeys).

2:11 hello

Listen and point to the story. Say. Color the children saying 'thank you'.
Language: lion, mouse; head, teeth; I'm hungry. I can help you! Thank you.

SOCIAL AND EMOTIONAL LEARNING

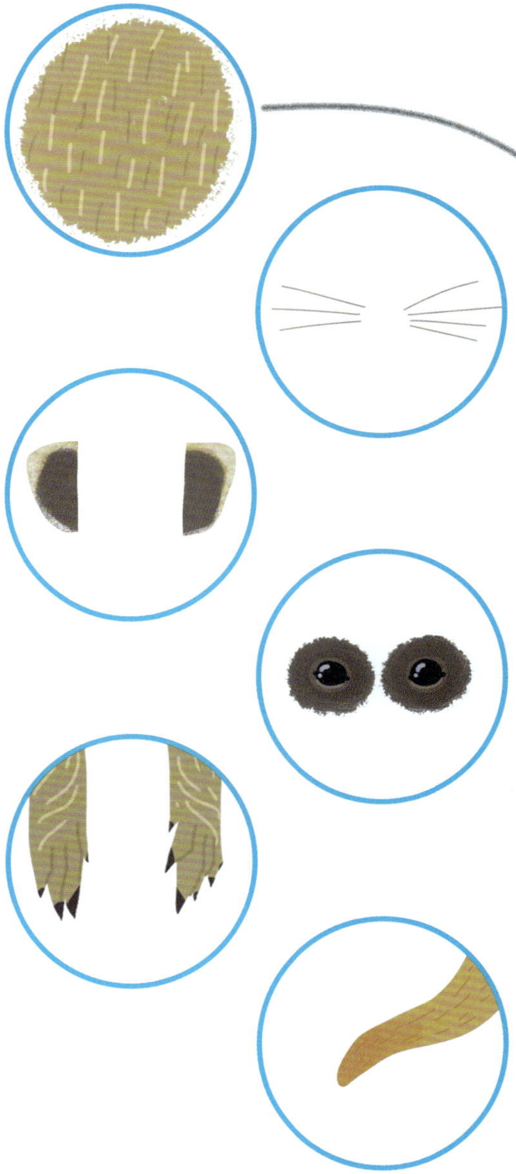

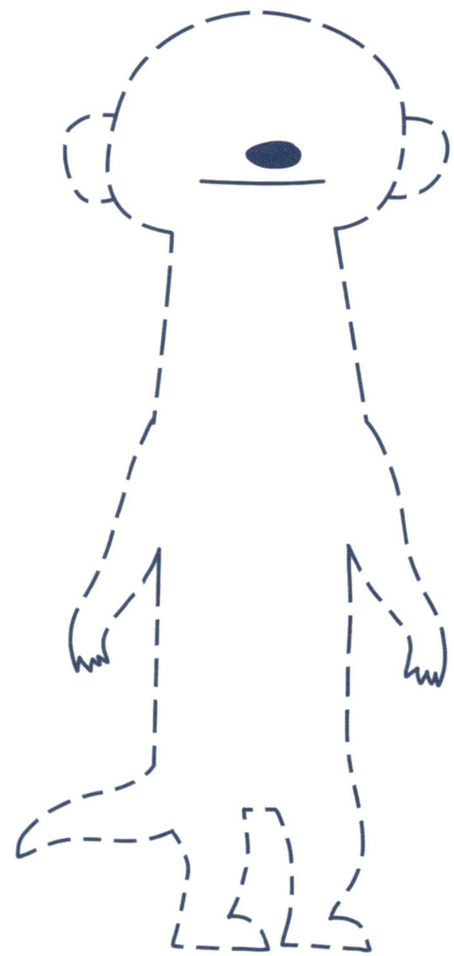

Listen and point. Match the parts of the body to the photo of a meerkat. Trace and complete the picture of a meerkat. Point and say. Language: claws, ears, eyes, fur, legs, nose, tail, whiskers; big, small; brown; What's that? It's (a meerkat). It has (big eyes).

Wild animals

Watch. Listen, point and sing *Five little monkeys*. Trace the numbers. Trace and color the monkeys. Say. **Language:** crocodile, monkey; numbers 1–5; (Five) little monkeys sitting in a tree. You can't catch me! Along comes Mr. Crocodile.

I can …

Vocabulary

Story

Speaking

Content

Color the circles of the animals you know. Listen, point and say. Listen and answer. Ask and say. Complete the faces to show what you can do. **Language:** crocodile, elephant, giraffe, hippo, lion, monkey, parrot, snake, tiger, zebra; What's that? It's (an elephant). It has (big ears). What are those? They're (monkeys).

Project

COOPERATIVE LEARNING

Choose, color and decorate a wild animal. Put your animals together to make a safari park mobile. Ask and say.
Language: crocodile, elephant, lion, zebra; numbers; colors; What's that? It's (a zebra). It's (black and white). It has (a tail). What are those? They're (lions). How many (elephants)? (Four). I like (the zebra). Do you like (the crocodile)? Yes. / No.

Daily routines

Giant Joe

2:16 2:17 2:18

Listen, point and repeat. Listen and stick the daily routine stickers. Listen and play *Memory*. Circle the daily routines you do more than once a day. Say. Language: brush my hair/teeth, get dressed, get up, wash my face/hands; blue, green, orange, pink, red, yellow

Language

2:19 2:20

Listen and find the new daily routines. Listen, point and sing *What do you do every day?* Check (✓) the routines in the song. Draw a routine. Ask and say. Language: brush my hair/teeth, get dressed, get up, have breakfast/lunch/dinner, take a shower, wash my face/hands; I (have lunch).

Story

1

2

3

4

5

6

2:22

Watch. Listen to the story *Giant Joe*. Circle what Grandpa's story is about. Stick the story sticker. Language: brush my hair/teeth, get dressed, get up, have breakfast/dinner, wash my face/hands; Do you (wash your hands)? Yes, I do. I (get up). It's time to (get dressed).

Story Song

Daily routines

Watch. Listen, point and sing *Giant Joe's day*. Circle the routines Giant Joe does every day. Ask and say.
Language: brush my hair/teeth, get dressed, get up, have breakfast/lunch/dinner, take a shower, wash my face/hands; I (brush my hair). Do you (wash your face)? Yes, I do. / No, I don't.

Daily routines

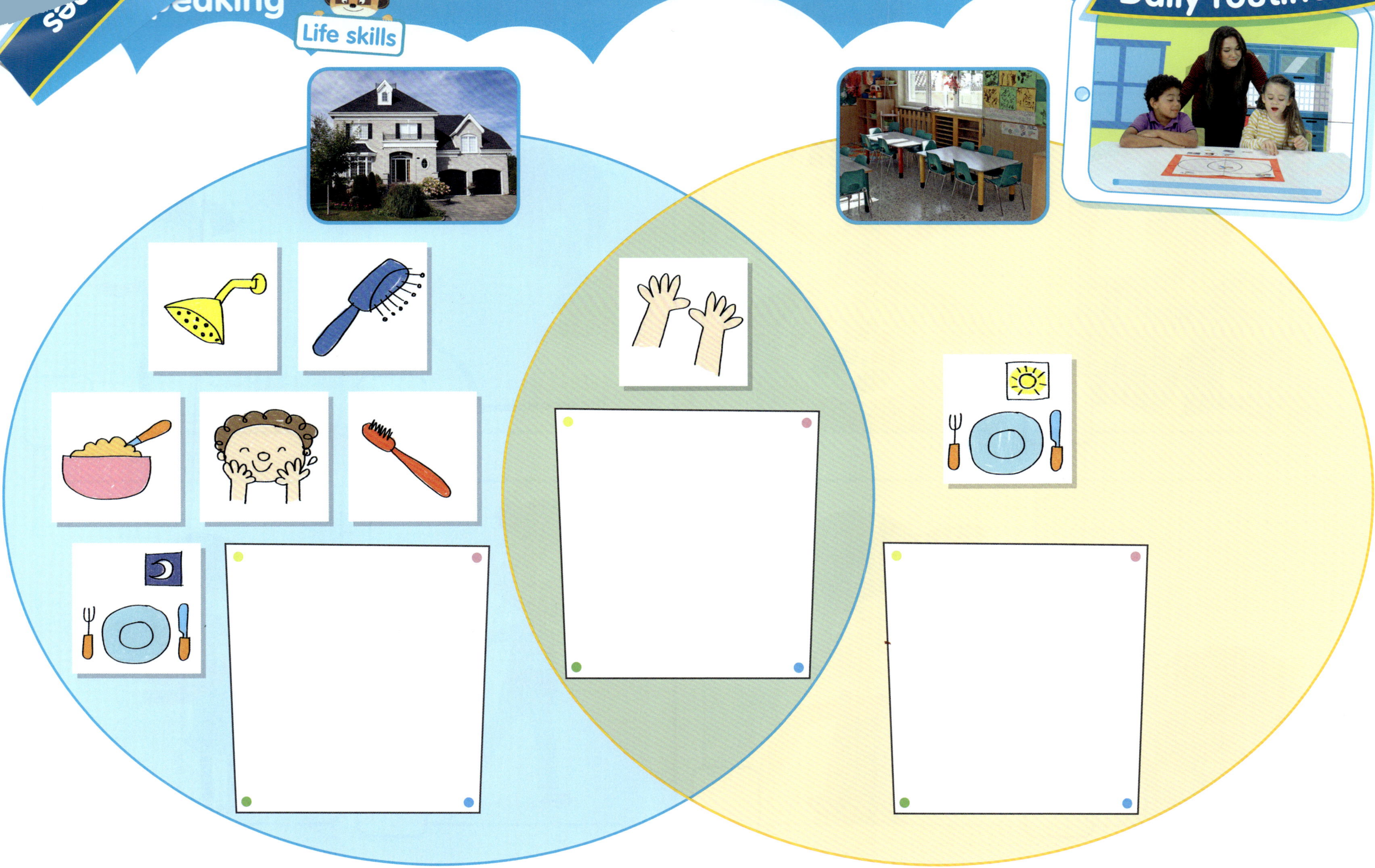

Watch. Listen and point. Draw three of your routines in the diagram. Ask and say. Language: brush my hair/teeth, have breakfast/lunch/dinner, take a shower, wash my face/hands; home, school; What do you do at (home)? I (have breakfast) at (home). I don't (have dinner) at (school). Do you (have lunch) at (school)? Yes. / No.

Lesson 6 Values Having a daily routine

2:26

hello

Listen, point and sing *I sleep, I eat, I learn, I play*. Check (✓) the daily routines you do. Say. Language: brush my teeth, drink water, eat, learn, play, sleep, take a shower, wash my hands; I (drink water) every day.

SOCIAL AND EMOTIONAL LEARNING

Daily routines

1 2 3 4

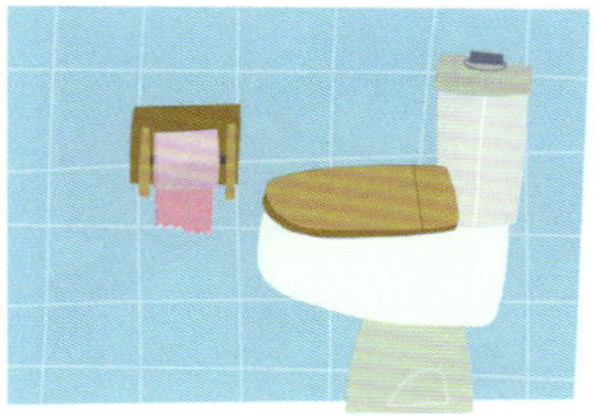

2:27

hello

Listen and point. Match and number the photos in order. Say. Circle the pictures to show when we need to wash our hands. Language: faucet, soap, towel, water; clean; wash my hands; numbers 1–4; I (wash my hands) with (soap).

Culture

Daily routines

2:28

hello

Watch. Listen and point to the story *Goldilocks and the three bears*. Draw and color a picture to show what you think happens next. Say. **Language:** bed, bowl, chair; big, small, tiny; Mommy, Daddy, Baby Bear; This (bowl) is (small).

Review

Daily routines

I can ...

Vocabulary

Story

Speaking

Content

Circle the routines you know. Listen, point and say. Listen and answer. Ask and say. Complete the faces to show what you can do. **Language:** brush my hair/teeth, get dressed, get up, have breakfast/lunch/dinner, take a shower, wash my face/hands; I (get up). I don't (have dinner). Do you (have lunch) at (home)?

Project

COOPERATIVE LEARNING

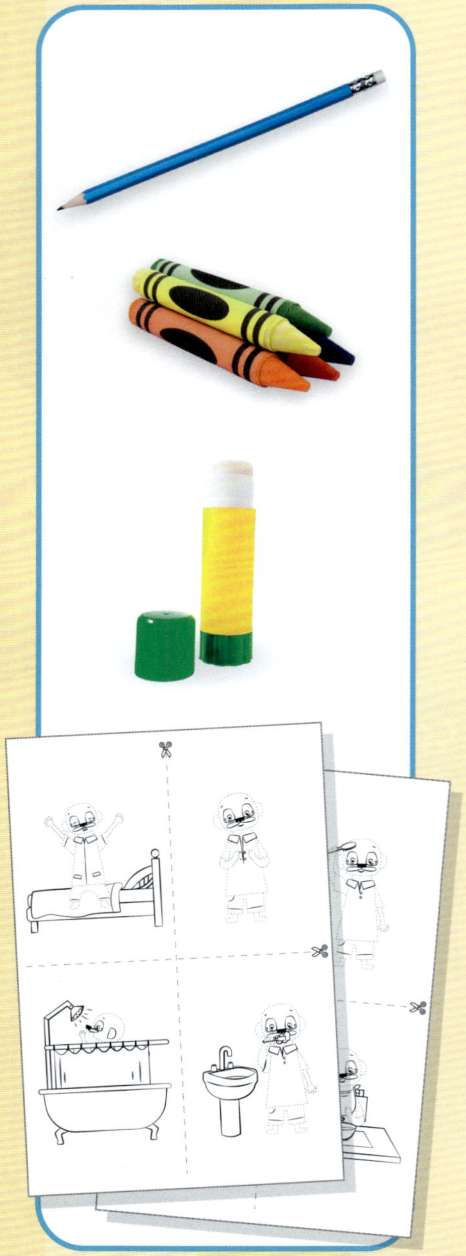

1

2

3

hello

Trace and color a picture of one of Giant Joe's daily routines. Put your pictures together to make a book, *Giant Joe's Day*. Ask and say. Language: brush my hair/teeth, get dressed, get up, have breakfast, take a shower, wash my face/hands; What do you do every day? I (get up). I don't (wash my face). Do you (get dressed)? Yes, I do. / No, I don't.

Meals

Toast, toast, toast!

Listen, point and repeat. Listen and stick the food stickers. Listen and play *Memory*. Circle the food you like. Say. Language: chicken, pancake, rice, salad, toast, yogurt; blue, green, orange, pink, red, yellow

Language

Listen and find the new food words. Listen, point and sing *What do you have for breakfast?* Match the food to Alex and Lucy. Ask and say. Language: chicken, fish, pancakes, pizza, rice, salad, soup, spaghetti, toast, yogurt; breakfast, lunch, dinner; What do you have for (dinner)? I have (soup).

Lesson 3

Story

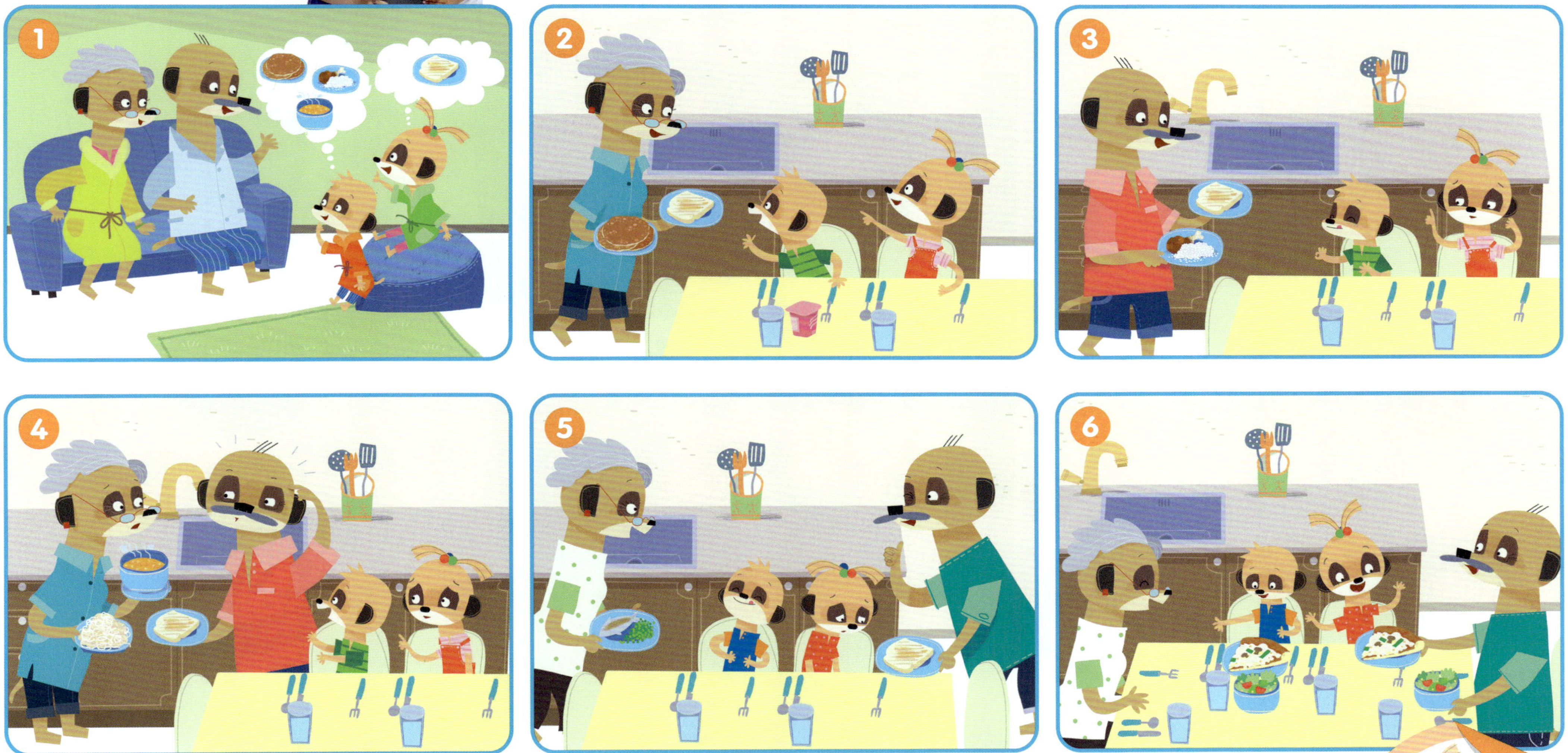

3:07

Watch. Listen to the story *Toast, toast, toast!* Circle the food Mimi wants for every meal. Stick the story sticker.

Language: chicken, fish, pancakes, peas, pizza, rice, salad, soup, spaghetti, toast, yogurt; breakfast, lunch, dinner; What do you have for (breakfast)? I have (yogurt). Do you want (pancakes)? I want (toast), please.

Story Song

Watch. Listen, point and sing *The toast song*. Circle 🙂 or ☹ to show the food Mimi wants and doesn't want. Ask and say. **Language:** chicken, pancakes, pizza, rice, salad, soup, spaghetti, toast, yogurt; Do you want (chicken)? Yes, please. / No, thank you. I want (toast). I don't want (chicken).

Watch. Listen and point. Match the characters to what they want for lunch. Draw a picture of what you want for lunch. Ask and say. Language: chicken, fish, pizza, rice, salad, spaghetti; Do you want (chicken)? Yes, please. / No, thank you. I want (fish). I don't want (pizza).

Lesson 6 Values Willingness to try food

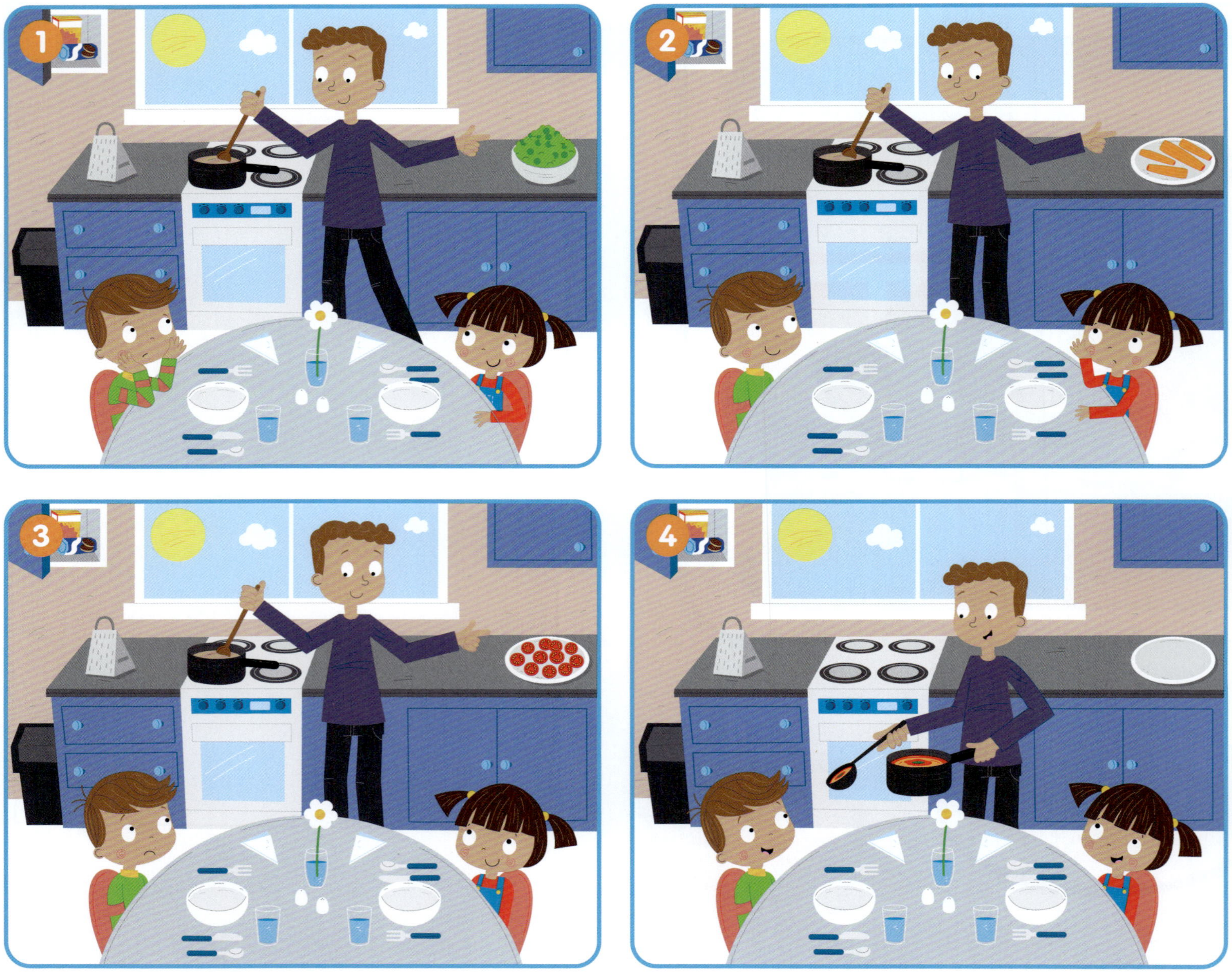

Listen and point to the story. Draw a picture of food you want to try. Ask and say.
Language: carrots, food, peas, soup, tomatoes; green, orange, red; Do you want (peas)? Yes, please. / No, thank you. I like (soup). I don't like (orange) food.

Content

3:12

Listen and point. Color the circles of the food that is good for you. Draw one more food that is good for you. Say. Language: fruit, vegetables; apples, bananas, candy, carrots, chips, cupcakes, ice cream, oranges, peas, plums, tomatoes; (Plums) are good for you. (Candy) isn't good for you. (Cupcakes) aren't good for you.

Culture

1 2 3 4 5

Watch. Listen, point and sing *Mix a pancake*. Match and number the pictures in order. Say. **Language:** pan, pancake; catch, cook, mix, toss; numbers 1–5; (Mix) the pancake.

Review

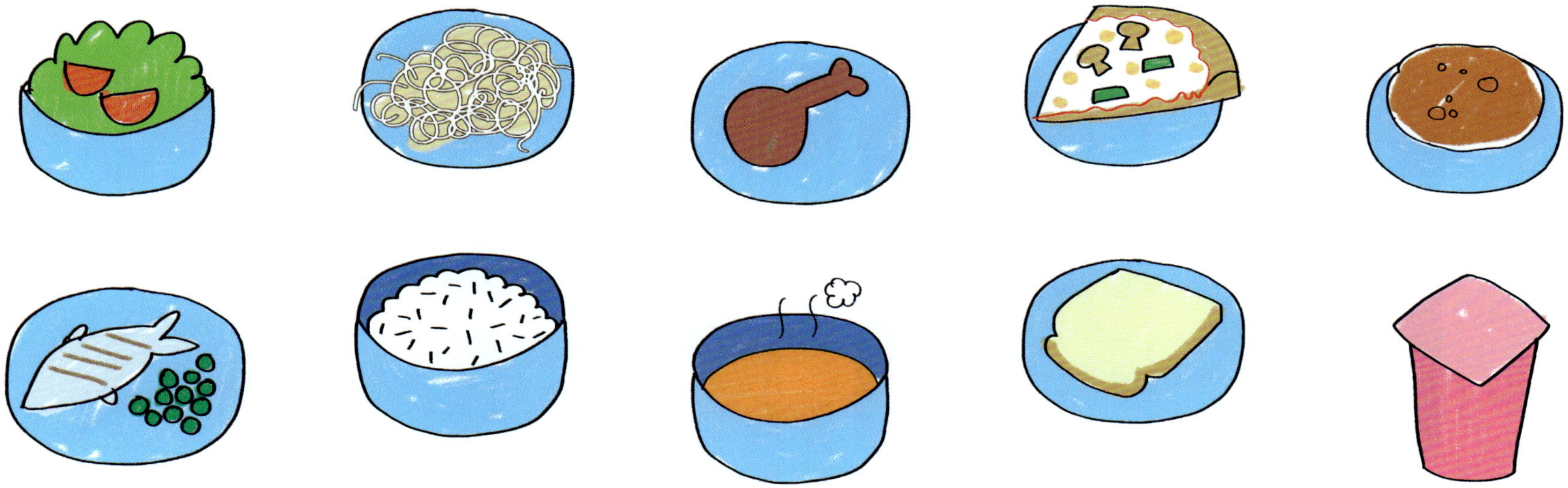

I can ...

Vocabulary

Story

Speaking

Content

Circle the food you know. Listen, point and say. Listen and answer. Ask and say. Complete the faces to show what you can do. Language: chicken, fish, pancake, pizza, rice, salad, soup, spaghetti, toast, yogurt; breakfast, lunch, dinner; What do you have for (lunch)? I have (rice). Do you want (soup)? Yes. / No.

Project

COOPERATIVE LEARNING

1

2

3

Make food that is good for you. Glue your food on plates. Ask and say. **Language:** carrots, chicken, fish, oranges, plums, salad, toast, yogurt; breakfast, lunch, dinner; (Yogurt) is good for you. (Carrots) are good for you. What do you have for (breakfast)? I have (toast). I like (spaghetti). I don't like (peas). Do you like (fish)? Yes, I do. / No, I don't.

Town

A day out

Listen, point and repeat. Listen and stick the town stickers. Listen and play *Memory*. Circle the places you go to. Say. Language: mall, movie theater, museum, swimming pool, toy store, zoo; blue, green, orange, pink, red, yellow

3:19 3:20 hello

Listen and find the new town words. Listen, point and sing *Do you want to go to the zoo?* Check (✓) where Alex and Lucy want to go. Ask and say. Language: bookstore, mall, movie theater, park, restaurant, supermarket, swimming pool, zoo; Do you want to go to (the zoo)? Yes. / No.

3:22

Watch. Listen to the story *A day out*. Circle the places Mimi and Dylan go to. Stick the story sticker.
Language: bookstore, mall, movie theater, museum, toy store; dinosaurs, space; Do you want to go to (the movie theater)? Yes, I do. / No, I don't. I want to go to (the museum). Let's go to (the mall).

Lesson 4 Story Song

Watch. Listen, point and sing *Dinosaurs in space.* Match Mimi and Dylan to what they want to do. Point and say. Draw a picture of something you want to learn about. Language: movie theater; books, dinosaurs, space, toys; go, learn, play, read; I want to play with (dinosaur) toys. I want to learn about (animals).

Speaking

Life skills

3:25

Watch. Listen and point. Match Alex and Lucy's pictures to the parts of the museum. Color the things you want to see. Ask and say. Language: dinosaur, fish, ocean, planet, space; museum; Do you want to see (the fish)? Yes. / No. Where do you want to go? I want to go to (a museum).

Lesson 6 Values Interest in learning

Listen, point and sing *I find out about my world*. Check (✓) the ways you learn. Draw a picture to show a way you like to learn. Say. Language: ask questions, find out about my world, go to school, look at books, play games, talk to friends, watch movies/TV; I want to learn. Do you?

SOCIAL AND EMOTIONAL LEARNING

Content

1 2 3 4

1

Listen and point. Match and number the photos to show how to cross the street safely. Say. **Language:** cars, crosswalk, sidewalk, stoplights, street; stop, look, listen; black, green, orange, red, white; numbers 1–4; The (stoplights) are (red).

Culture

Watch. Listen and point to the story *The enormous carrot*. Color the things in the story. Say. **Language:** carrot; boy, girl, man, woman; pull; Do you want to help? Yes, of course. The (man) pulls the (woman).

Review

I can ...

Vocabulary

Story

Speaking

Content

Circle the town words you know. Listen, point and say. Listen and answer. Ask and say. Complete the faces to show what you can do. Language: bookstore, mall, movie theater, museum, park, restaurant, supermarket, swimming pool, toy store, zoo; Do you want to go to (the zoo)? Yes, I do. / No, I don't. I want to go to (the park).

Project

COOPERATIVE LEARNING

1

2

3

Choose and color a place. Put the places together to make a map of Mimi's town. Ask and say. **Language:** bookstore, movie theater, park, restaurant, supermarket, swimming pool, toy store, zoo; Where do you want to go? I want to go to (the supermarket). I don't want to go to (the restaurant). Do you want to go to (the zoo)? Do you like (the toy store)? Yes, I do. / No, I don't. I like (the park).

hello

Music
Mimi's band

Vocabulary Lesson 1

Listen, point and repeat. Listen and stick the music stickers. Listen and play *Memory*. Circle the musical instruments you like. Say. Language: drum, guitar, maracas, piano, recorder, tambourine; blue, green, orange, pink, red, yellow

Listen and find the new music words. Listen, point and sing *Listen, clap, dance!* Check (✓) the things Alex and Lucy are doing in the song. Ask and say. Language: drum, guitar, piano, recorder, tambourine; clap, dance, listen, sing; What are you doing? I'm (playing the piano). I'm (singing).

Story

Watch. Listen to the story *Mimi's band*. Circle the musical instruments in the class show. Stick the story sticker. **Language:** drum, maracas, piano, recorder, tambourine; sing; What are you doing? I'm (playing the recorder). Do you like (playing the maracas)? Yes, I do. / No, I don't.

Lesson 4 Story Song

Watch. Listen, point and sing *Welcome to our show*. Follow and draw the paths through the maze to show what the characters are doing in the show. Ask and say. **Language:** drum, maracas, recorder, tambourine; clap, dance, listen, sing; What are you doing? I'm (playing the recorder). I'm (singing).

Lesson 5

Speaking

Life skills

Watch. Listen and point. Match Auntie Vicky, Alex and Lucy to the instrument they like playing. Circle the instrument(s) you like playing. Ask and say. **Language:** drum, guitar, maracas, piano, recorder, tambourine; Do you like (playing the guitar)? Yes, I do. / No, I don't. I like (playing the drum).

Values Willingness to practice

1

2

3

4

4:11

hello

Listen and point to the story. Color the pictures of things you practice. Ask and say.

Language: piano, recorder; practice; What are you doing? I'm (playing the recorder). I'm (practicing).

SOCIAL AND EMOTIONAL LEARNING

1 2 3 4

1

Listen and point. Clap the rhythm. Number the pictures in order. Color the circle of your favorite rhythm. Say. **Language:** fast, slow, loud, quiet; numbers 1–4; It's (loud). Clap the rhythm.

Music

Watch. Listen, point and sing *I am the music man*. Trace the instruments. Color your favorite instrument. Ask and say. Language: drum, piano, trombone, violin; What can you play? I play the (violin).

Review

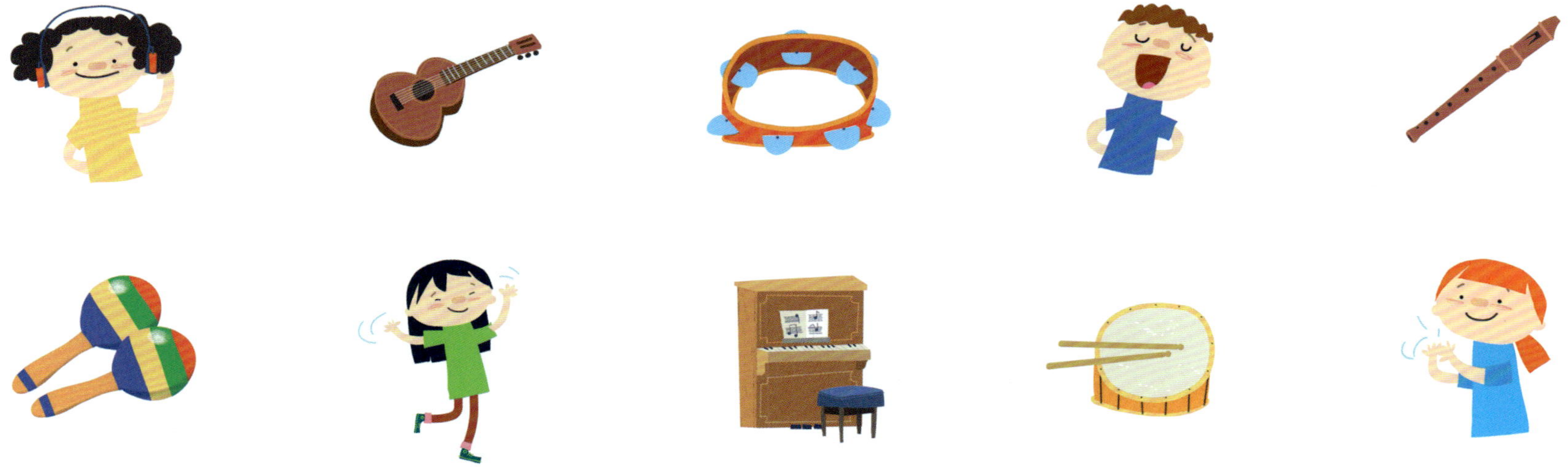

I can ...

Vocabulary

Story

Speaking

Content

Circle the music words you know. Listen, point and say. Listen and answer. Ask and say. Complete the faces to show what you can do. Language: drum, guitar, maracas, piano, recorder, tambourine; clap, dance, listen, sing; What are you doing? I'm (playing the piano). Do you like (playing the drum)? I like (playing the guitar).

COOPERATIVE LEARNING

Make and decorate maracas. Play your maracas together and invent a rhythm. Ask and say. Language: maracas; loud, quiet, fast, slow; colors; What are you doing? I'm playing my (maracas). Do you like playing your (maracas)? Yes, I do. / No, I don't. My maracas are (red and blue). I like the (green) maracas. I like playing my (maracas).

Bugs
Honey for dinner

4:16 hello 4:17 4:18

Listen, point and repeat. Listen and stick the bug stickers. Listen and play *Memory*. Circle the bugs you sometimes see. Say. Language: ant, bee, butterfly, ladybug, snail, worm; blue, green, orange, pink, red, yellow

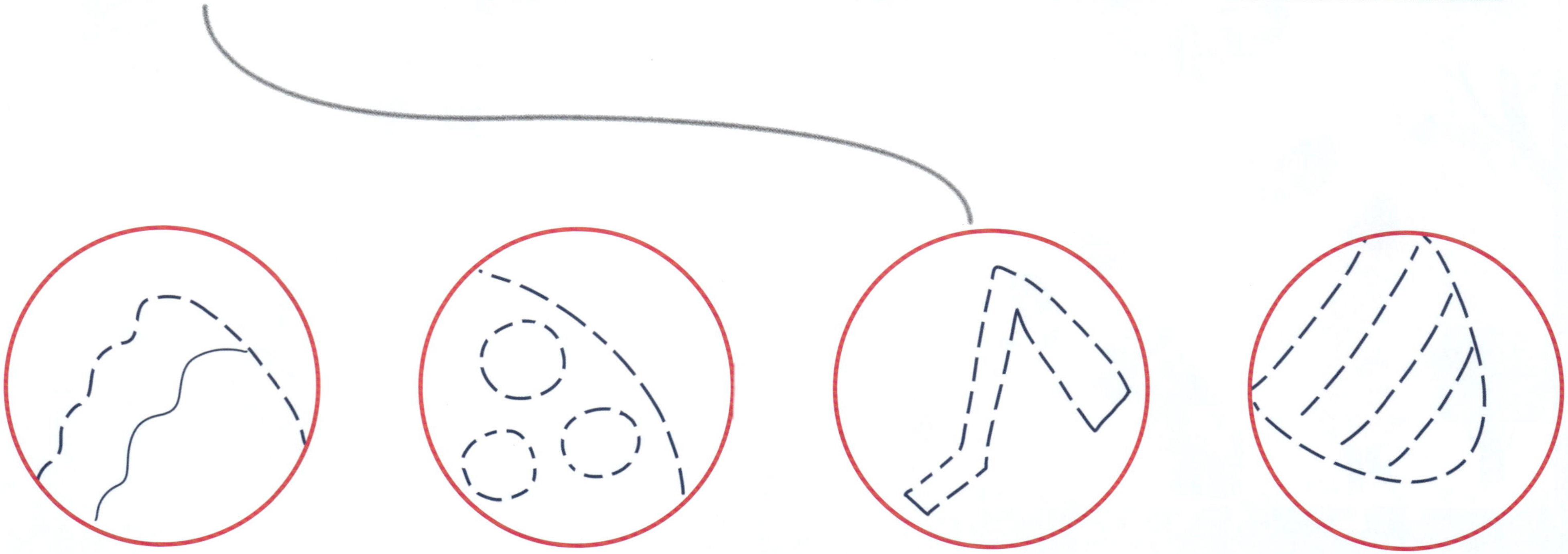

Listen and find the new bug words. Listen, point and sing *Does a butterfly have wings?* Match the bugs to the pictures. Trace and color. Ask and say. Language: ant, bee, butterfly, ladybug; legs, spots, stripes, wings; Does a (snail) have (spots)? Yes, it does. / No, it doesn't.

Lesson 3 Story

4:22

Watch. Listen to the story *Honey for dinner.* Circle the bug who knows where the bees are. Stick the story sticker. Language: bee, butterfly, ladybug, snail, worm; legs, spots, stripes, wings; colors; A (ladybug)'s (red and black). It has (spots). Does it have (legs)? Yes, it does. / No, it doesn't.

Story Song

Watch. Listen, point and sing *We want to get some honey*. Follow and draw a path through the maze. Color the bugs. Ask and say. Language: bee, butterfly, ladybug, snail, worm; Where are (the bees)? I don't know. Ask (the ladybug), please.

Lesson 5

Speaking

Life skills

Bugs

1 2 3 4

Watch. Listen and point. Name the bugs. Number the photos in order. Invent and draw a bug. Ask and say. **Language:** bee, ladybug, snail, worm; legs, spots, stripes, wings; colors; numbers 1–4; Does it have (legs)? Yes, it does. / No, it doesn't. It has (wings). It doesn't have (stripes). It's (black and yellow).

Little Book of Values

4:26

hello

Listen, point and sing *I care for our world*. Color the frames of the pictures that show things you care for. Draw a picture of you caring for something. Say.
Language: animals, bugs, family, flowers, friends, nature, trees; I care for (nature).

SOCIAL AND EMOTIONAL LEARNING

1 2 3 4

1

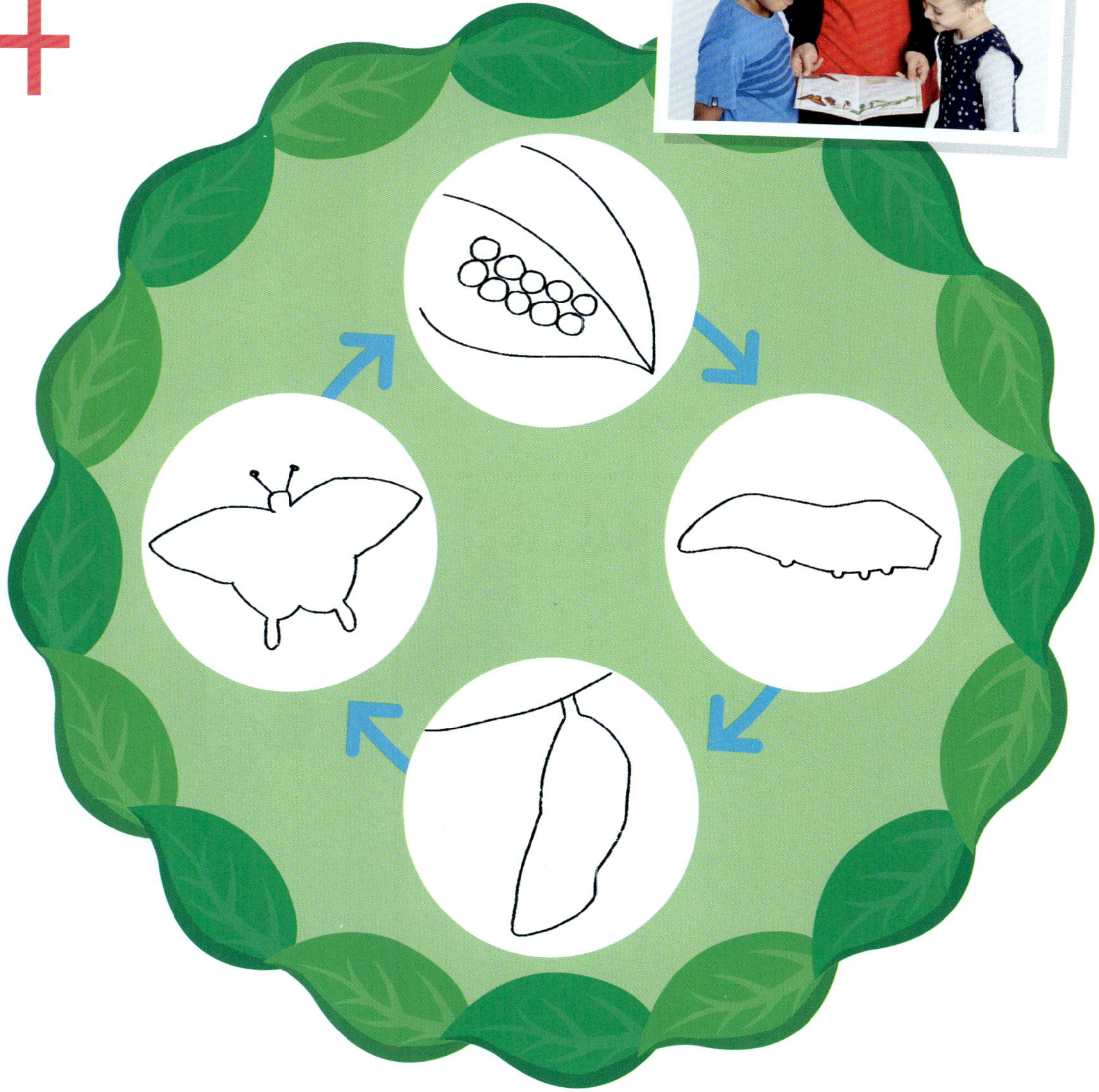

4:27

hello

Listen and point. Number the stages in the life cycle of a butterfly. Draw and color the pictures of the life cycle. Say. **Language:** butterfly, caterpillar, chrysalis, egg, leaf; numbers 1–4; They're eggs on a leaf.

Culture

Watch. Listen and point to the story *The ant and the grasshopper*. Draw a picture to show what you think happens next. Say. **Language:** ant, grasshopper; summer, winter; happy, hungry, sad; play, work; food; I want to (play). I'm (hungry). I have (food). I don't have (food).

Review

I can ...

Vocabulary

Story

Speaking

Content

Color the circles of the bug words you know. Listen, point and say. Listen and answer. Ask and say. Complete the faces to show what you can do. Language: ant, bee, butterfly, ladybug, snail, worm; legs, spots, stripes, wings; Does it have (spots)? Yes, it does. / No, it doesn't. It has (stripes). It doesn't have (legs).

Project

COOPERATIVE LEARNING

1

2

3

Make a bug. Put your bugs together to make a diorama. Ask and say. Language: ant, bee, butterfly, ladybug, snail, worm; legs, spots, stripes, wings; colors; Does it have (legs)? Yes, it does. / No, it doesn't. It has (wings). It doesn't have (legs). It's (red and black). I like (the butterfly). Do you like (the snail)? Yes, I do. / No, I don't.

Colors

Listen, point and say. Color the animals the same as in the pictures. Color the circle of your favorite animal. Say. **Language:** black, blue, gray, red, white, yellow; It's (red).

Listen, point and say. Complete the pattern. Create your own color pattern. Say.
Language: brown, gray, green, orange, pink, purple; It's (orange).

Numbers 10 20 30 40 50 60 70 80 90 100

Listen, point and say. Draw lines to connect the numbers in order. Circle your favorite number. Say.
Language: numbers 10–100; It's (forty).

Numbers

5 10 15 20 25 30 35 40 45 50

4:34

hello

Listen, point and say. Match the missing numbers. Say.
Language: numbers 1–50; It's (fifteen).

Shapes

Listen, point and say. Draw and color the next shape in the sequence. Say.
Language: circle, diamond, oval, rectangle, square, star, triangle; It's a (star).

Shapes

1 2 3 4 5 6 7 8 9 10

4:35

hello

Listen, point and say. Count the shapes in the picture. Circle the number and match it to the correct shape. Say. **Language:** circle, diamond, oval, rectangle, square, star, triangle; numbers 1–10; I can see (three) (diamonds).

Concepts

Listen, point and say. Circle the pictures of hungry children red. Circle the pictures of thirsty children blue. Say.
Language: hungry, thirsty; I'm (hungry).

Concepts

Listen, point and say. Find and circle six differences in the pictures that show clean and dirty. Say.
Language: clean, dirty; It's (clean).

Concepts

Listen, point and say. Match the old people and animals to the young ones. Draw a picture of someone old or young in your family. Say.
Language: old, young; He's/She's/It's (old).

Festivals

World Book Day

Listen, point and say. Listen and sing *We love books.* Match the books. Choose and color the cover of the book you like best. Say. Language: animals, people, pictures, stories, words, world; I like books about (people). I like books with (pictures).

World Animal Day

Listen, point and say. Listen and sing *Save the rhino*. Find and circle the animals in the song. Draw and color an animal you want to save. Say.
Language: elephant, gorilla, panda, polar bear, rhino, tiger; Save the (panda).

Festivals

World Environment Day

1

2

3

4

Listen, point and say. Listen and sing *When we go to the countryside*. Number the pictures in the order of the song. Draw a picture of you in the places you go to. Say. **Language:** beach, countryside, forest, mountains; I go to the (countryside). Let's protect the (beach).